◆

And all of you, whole a
maybe you are still wo
and you write by quill.
I am almost, of the volcano.

mpT
MODERN POETRY IN TRANSLATION
The best of world poetry

No. 3 2024

© *Modern Poetry in Translation* 2024 and contributors

ISSN (print) 0969-3572
ISSN (online) 2052-3017
ISBN (print) 978-1-910485-40-8

Editor: Janani Ambikapathy
Managing Editor: Sarah Hesketh
Digital Content Editor: Ed Cottrell
Finance Manager: Deborah de Kock
Marketing & Communications
Assistant: Chloe Eliott

Design by Brett Evans Biedscheid
Cover Art by Pau Gasol Valls
Typesetting by Libanus Press
Proofreading by Katy Evans-Bush

Printed and bound in Great Britain by Typecast Colour, Kent
For submissions and subscriptions please visit
www.modernpoetryintranslation.com

Modern Poetry in Translation Limited. A Company Limited by Guarantee
Registered in England and Wales, Number 5881603 UK
Registered Charity Number 1118223

Cover description: A transparent green tunnel stretches across the page, from
the top right section winding round to the bottom. The tunnel is held up by
wooden scaffolding, contrasted against a cloudy sky. Inside the tubes are four
opaque human figures, in various states of sliding down. At the same time, a
black and yellow fox gingerly climbs up the outside of the tunnel.

Above: On the left, the Arts Council England logo curves around in a circle,
next to a black outline of a hand crossing fingers. Underneath both images,
'LOTTERY FUNDED' is written. In a line on the right, the text reads,
'Supported using public funding by ARTS COUNCIL ENGLAND'.
On the right, the institut ramon llull logo has four black curved lines and
the text reads 'institut ramon llull

MODERN POETRY IN TRANSLATION

Your language anticipating mine
Focus on Catalan

CONTENTS

Editorial **1**
Guest editorial by Ronald Puppo

KAROLINE BRÆNDJORD, two poems **7**
Translated by RACHEL RANKIN from Norwegian

ANJA KAMPMANN, 'mole' **10**
Translated by ADAM TAPPER from German

CLEMENTINA SUÁREZ, 'The Prayer' **12**
Translated by JP ALLEN from Spanish

ÁLVARO FAUSTO TARUMA, two poems **17**
Translated by GRANT AZEVEDO BELEZA-SCHUTZMAN
    from Portuguese

ROXANA CRISÓLOGO, 'Here we pay homage to Peruvian beauty' **20**
Translated by KIM JENSEN and JUDITH SANTOPIETRO from Spanish

ERIK SOLVANGER, three poems from *Why Life Goes Faster* **23**
    in a White Coat
Translated by ASTRID ALBEN from Dutch

DOROTHEA GRÜNZWEIG, 'wound bed in the weteli woods' **27**
Translated by DERK WYNAND from German

OSIP MANDELSTAM, three poems **31**
Translated by TONY BRINKLEY from Russian

JEAN D'AMÉRIQUE, 'Wounded Bird' **35**
Translated by AIDAN ROONEY from French

SAKTHI JOTHI, 'Liberation' **39**
Translated by THILA VARGHESE from Tamil

VASYL STUS, from 'Streams' **42**
Translated by BOHDAN TOKARSKYI and NINA MURRAY from Ukrainian

GUNNAR, 'Threat' **45**
Translated by KLEIN VOORHEES from German

CEVAHIR BEDEL, three poems **47**
Translated by JEFFREY KAHRS and METE ÖZEL from Turkish

Focus

GEMMA GORGA, two poems **53**
Translated by SHARON DOLIN from Catalan

ÀXEL SANJOSÉ, two poems **56**
Translated by RICHARD DOVE from Catalan

ANNA GUAL, two poems **59**
Translated by AKAISER from Catalan

JOSEP CHECA, two poems **63**
Translated by RONALD PUPPO from Catalan

TÒNIA PASSOLA, 'Desire' **66**
Translated by RONALD PUPPO from Catalan

SÍLVIA AYMERICH-LEMOS, two poems **68**
Translated by MATTHEW GEDEN from Catalan

SÍLVIA AYMERICH-LEMOS, 'Alghero' **71**
Translated by KATHLEEN MCNERNEY and
    SÍLVIA AYMERICH-LEMOS from Catalan

FELÍCIA FUSTER, 'And More II' **73**
Translated by MARIALENA CARR from Catalan

JOSEP CARNER, two poems   77
Translated by NIALL O'GALLAGHER from Catalan

MARIA-MERCÈ MARÇAL, two poems   80
Translated by CLYDE MONEYHUN from Catalan

GABRIEL FERRATER, two poems   83
Translated by ADRIAN NATHAN WEST from Catalan

MARIA ANTÒNIA SALVÀ, two poems   87
Translated by CLYDE MONEYHUN from Catalan

MERCÈ RODOREDA, two poems   90
Translated by REBECCA SIMPSON from Catalan

JOSEP LLUÍS AGUILÓ, 'The Sun Tree'   93
Translated by ANNA CROWE from Catalan

MIQUEL MARTÍ I POL, three poems   97
Translated by LOURDES MANYÉ and WAYNE COX from Catalan

Reviews

PHƯƠNG ANH NGUYỄN Scent of the Birthsoil   101
On Chronicles of a Village, Nguyễn Thanh Hiện,
tr. by Quyên Nguyễn-Hoàng

KHADIJA AIDOO Rhythms of the Soul   104
On Solio, Samira Negrouche, tr. by Nancy Naomi Carlson

Notes on Contributors   108

EDITORIAL

by Janani Ambikapathy and Ronald Puppo

Most of the work in this issue – except the section on Catalan
poetry – was selected by the previous editor, Khairani Barokka,
and the interim editor, Sarah Hesketh. I'm very grateful to them
for putting together an excellent selection of poems including the
works of Clementina Suárez, Jean D'Amérique and Gunnar, for
commissioning reviews on the works of Nguyễn Thanh Hiện and
Samira Negrouche.

I have especially to thank the translator and scholar, Ronald
Puppo, for helping me curate the section on Catalan poetry.
Given Puppo's expertise, I'll let him take us through a brief history
of Catalan poetics. The selection here is not representative in
any sense – it is merely a glimpse into an undeniably vast and
beautiful canon.

– *Janani Ambikapathy*

A Language of Life

The literary origins of Catalan are mediaeval and – not unlike
those of other Romance languages – take solid form with writers
whose important works appear in the vernacular. Among the most
influential of mediaeval writers in Catalan were the celebrated
Mallorcan philosopher and theologian Ramon Llull; Andreu Febrer,
poet and author of the first known verse translation of *La Divina
Commedia* in Europe; Ausiàs March, the remarkable poet and
knight-adventurer from Valencia; and Joanot Martorell, the
Valencian author of the acclaimed late mediaeval chivalric novel
Tirant lo Blanc.

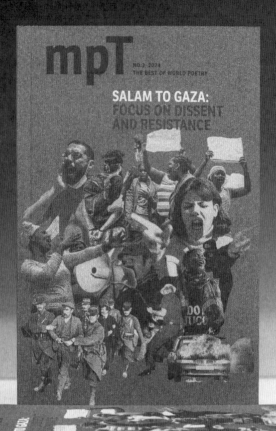

Catalan literary production's mediaeval heyday decelerated during the early modern period, only to jump-start with the nineteenth-century burst of vitality that flung open the gates to an astonishing recovery known as the Catalan Renaixença. Romantic poet and rebel priest Jacint Verdaguer penned the groundbreaking modern foundational epics of the Iberian nations, *L'Atlàntida* (Atlantis), and of Catalonia, *Canigó* (Mount Canigó), both praised highly and translated throughout Europe. Concurrently, Canary-born playwright Àngel Guimerà elevated Catalan theatre to international success with his Romantic tragedy *Mar i cel*, translated and performed widely; his modern classic, *Terra baixa*, known in English as *Marta of the Lowlands*, garnered itinerant performances in the US and was produced as a drama film directed by J. Searle Dawley, released in 1914 by Paramount Pictures.

Literary and artistic tides shifted as turn-of-the-century trends spawned what would be dubbed Catalan modernism – Modernisme – spearheaded by outstanding poet Joan Maragall; by novelists Raimon Casellas and Caterina Albert (aka Víctor Català); by painters Santiago Rusiñol and Ramon Casas; and by architects Lluís Domènech i Montaner and, most famously, Antoni Gaudí. Along with literary output, the power of the written word was strengthened in the early twentieth century by the milestone efforts of Catalan lexicographers and grammarians such as Antoni Maria Alcover and Pompeu Fabra, followed later by Francesc de B. Moll and Joan Coromines. Meanwhile, throughout the twentieth century, the inventory of titles published in Catalan skyrocketed through the tireless efforts of translators importing major-language works from ancient classics to contemporary worldwide bestsellers.

Reciprocally, however, translations of original Catalan output into other languages, especially English, faced considerable hurdles.

ATLANTIS

by Jacint Verdaguer

Translated from Catalan by Ronald Puppo

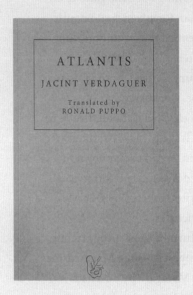

Atlantis was the giant at war with all
Olympus; arching the rising and setting suns;
but not content with all the earth for hall,
she sought the very stars to crown her front.

The rolling Thunder's razing flame expelled
her from her high-flung stair and plunged her deep
beneath the fiery waves and sulphur's meld
amid the jetsam on the boiling sea.

A majestic, epic poem and lasting jewel of Catalan literary tradition, *Atlantis* displays both colossal architecture and a descriptive power that creates memorable passages of prodigious beauty, from the vision of the garden of the Hesperides to the dream of Queen Isabel. *Atlantis* was the forging work of modern literary Catalan, and earned Verdaguer recognition in and outside of Catalonia. Today, it remains an essential part of both the Catalan and European literary canons.

The translation is 'a labour of love by Ronald Puppo, who has miraculously managed to match the assonance and rhymes of Verdaguer's stanzas. It reads beautifully.'   —Michael Eaude, *Catalonia Today*

Fum d'Estampa Press Ltd   https://www.fumdestampa.com
ISBN: 9781913744250

Poet and pioneering translator David H. Rosenthal succeeded remarkably in turning Martorell's *Tirant lo Blanc* into an English-language bestseller (New York: Schocken Books, 1984; London: Macmillan, 1984; Baltimore: John Hopkins University Press, 1996). In addition, Rosenthal Englished, among others, Caterina Albert's landmark classic *Solitude*, Joan Perucho's *Natural History*, and several of Mercè Rodoreda's important works, including her signature novel *The Time of the Doves* (*La Plaça del Diamant*), translated into more than thirty-five languages. Other notable pioneering scholars and translators who laboured to bring Catalan literature to English-language readers include, among others, Joan Gili, Pearse Hutchinson, Arthur Terry, D. Sam Abrams, and Kathleen McNerney. English-language publishers on both sides of the Atlantic have often given crucial support, and have grown in number in recent decades, springboarding Catalan authors into the contemporary spotlight, especially since 2007, when Catalan culture was the guest of honour at the Frankfurt Book Fair. Major support from the Institut Ramon Llull has been vital, not to mention recognition and dissemination of Catalan authors and their translators by the Anglo-Catalan Society and the North American Catalan Society. All this has led to the success of high-profile translators of Catalan narrative such as Peter Bush, Mara Faye Lethem, and Martha Tennent; and of Catalan poetry by Anna Crowe, Kristine Doll, and Christopher Whyte, to name just a few.

The task of the translator of poetry, it has been said, is an impossible one. Vladimir Nabokov famously contended that the best approach was to go absolutely literal, with footnotes rising up the page like skyscrapers; but to strip a text of its poetic packaging would be to render it voiceless. Salvaging the voice – giving new voice to the otherly voice – means repackaging the poem in translation with a view to re-creating the form–content synthesis. A tall order! The poem in translation is, of course, a new text. The translator – author and voice-giver of the new text – must negotiate shifting interlingual denotation and connotation; must strike a delicate balance between the canonic and the colloquial; must blend lyricism and imagery while releasing subtle phonic effects and rhythms. George Steiner has remarked that 'translation is the donation of being across space and time.' The textual and contextual transformation that is translation becomes a catalyst for encounter beyond the cultural self.

Poetry has been called the language of life. Catalan, as this selection of poems makes clear, is very much alive – a language of life. What better way to embrace a language of life than in the language of life.

KAROLINE BRÆNDJORD

Translated by Rachel Rankin from Norwegian

Can one ever reconcile oneself to being abandoned? Where can one turn when a mother takes her own life? How can we accept that which cannot be accepted? And how do we behave in nature when nature cannot understand us?

These are the questions addressed by Karoline Brændjord in her award-winning, critically acclaimed debut poetry collection *Jeg vil våkne til verden* [I Want to Wake Up to the World], published in 2020. Drawing on personal experience, Brændjord explores the aftermath of a mother's suicide and the grief of an abandoned daughter. In Brændjord's poems, recurring themes and images of nature guide the reader through a journey of mourning and acceptance where grief, joy and nature are intertwined.

'Light,' the opening poem of the collection, serves as an effective introduction to these themes as it juxtaposes the mournful – that is, grief – with the positive image of light, thereby depicting grief as something that illuminates and brings clarity: 'Grief turns everything to light'. 'Elm' continues these themes by drawing comparisons between personal grief and the loss of leaves on an elm tree, thus highlighting the relationship between death and the natural world: 'This separation is never ceremonial, never | tragic. It is commonplace. Ask the elm about loss'.

Jeg vil våkne til verden won both the 2020 Norwegian Critics Prize for Literature and the 2020 Tarjei Vesaas Prize for Debut Writers and was considered by many critics to be one of the best Norwegian books of 2020.

Light

Toil turns everything to light. Grief turns everything to light.
I was born and light shone from my parents' faces.
When I laugh, my mother lights up,
when I set the table, my father lights up,
when I pour wine into glasses, I light up the world.

I grow and the light flows out through my fingers.
I go to the brook to collect water. The brook is light.
And the water I bring back with me is light.
Everything I touch: birchbark, grass,
a butterfly, potato sprouts, milk and a stake.

My body is a message.
I grow beneath the heavens in flesh and wonder.
I cast the light of wonder across the land.
All my questions flood like light from my mouth.
When I ask the anemone its name, it turns white.

Come to me in my world of light
with golden fields and sparkling streams.
I tread a path with my childlike steps.
My words are lights. My stories are lights.
My longings are lights. I'm the brightest light in the world.

Elm

The one who sits patiently will see the forest transform, see
the leaves of an elm unfold themselves and later curl
in on themselves. The patient one will see the tree let go, its grip
on the leaf so feeble and weak that a mere breath of wind will
set the leaf free. This separation is never ceremonial, never
tragic. It is commonplace. Ask the elm about loss.

ANJA KAMPMANN

Translated by Adam Tapper from German

Anja Kampmann's poem appeals with its unique shape, irregular line breaks and unconventional spacing. Kampmann's use of metaphor, her evocative and nostalgic language, and her ability to seamlessly comment on both the present and the past capture the reader's imagination.

The poem's narrator toggles between memories of the eradication of 'moles', at first the garden rodents and then more ominously, brain cancer cells. The narrator remembers the relative ease of digging moles out from the meadow using shovels and pitchforks, often unearthing baby moles with 'paws not yet blackened'. As the mole problem intensifies, they resort to electronic pest repellers 'stabbed into the earth' to drive the moles away with sound waves. The innocent meadow adventures take a dark turn as the reader realises that it will not be possible to stop nature's course. Kampmann frets over the moles 'feasting and rummaging under the earth', now speaking not of garden moles but of cancer cells feeding on and multiplying within the brain, exploiting a different set of complex, hidden passageways. Electrodes like those in the garden are implanted in the partner's skull, reaching into the 'pitch black earth of [their] brain' to deliver 'waves' and 'small shocks' to attack the cancer cells.

The German word for *mole*, the garden animal (*Maulwurf*) differs from the word for *mole*, a suspicious growth that could signal cancer (*Muttermal*). In the English translation, the final lines 'where you could talk about moles | and know what you were dealing with' take on a new degree of interest through the double entendre created by a single English word with two distinct meanings.

mole

we used to lift them out from the meadows
with pitchforks, spades
rosy snout and burrowing, paws not yet blackened
soft skin plowing through the meadows.
then came the metal rods
that were stabbed into the earth

                for sound waves

a distinct rhythm
to drive them away from their tunnels.

the deep sleep
the feasting and rummaging
under the earth
              now you wear two electrodes on your head
they reach a finger's length into the pitch black earth
of your brain
        where they send out waves, small shocks
into a nameless system of passageways
                  shallows
with the name of a sickness. hardly any more.

the meadow was crisscrossed with hills
somewhere in the dark, a beetle was cracked
an earthworm
consumed.   those were   the good times

where you could talk about moles
and know what you were dealing with.

CLEMENTINA SUÁREZ

Translated by JP Allen from Spanish

U.S. scholar Janet Gold calls Clementina Suárez (1902-91) 'the
legendary matriarch of Honduran letters, [who] scandalised
Central American society with her bohemian lifestyle, her passionate
woman-centred poetry, and her dedicated and unconventional
promotion of art and literature'.

Born in Tegucigalpa, Honduras, Suárez lived in Mexico, Cuba,
and El Salvador, before returning to Honduras later in life. Her
10 collections embrace half a century and an expansive array of
themes, united by her energetic, distinctive voice. Best known
as a poet, Suárez also organised creative communities of writers,
painters, political dissidents, friends, and admirers.

Given Suárez's stature and contemporary relevance, her work is
under-translated. Janet Gold's rigorous, beautiful 1992 biography,
Clementina Suárez: Her Life and Poetry, includes full translations of
some poems and excerpts from others. However, almost none
of Suárez's hundreds of poems have appeared in translation.

I first read Suárez's name in passing. In urging solidarity with
Central American migrants, an op-ed in a Mexican newspaper
(which I've since been unable to find) reminded readers that any
young person making the dangerous journey could be 'the next
Pablo Neruda or Clementina Suárez'. I was surprised and ashamed
that I'd never heard of her. What started as a simple effort to educate
myself about a notable author turned into a deep admiration for
her work.

I'm grateful for Janet Gold's mentorship and support, to Frances
Simán for connecting me with the Suárez family, and to Alba Rosa
Suárez for generously granting permission to translate her
mother's work.

The Prayer

But, God! I am not like the oak
branch, forever at peace.

I am not like sandalwood, which has never
changed its scent;
I do not love immutable things
like the enormous boulder in the path,
like eternal silence,
like infinity.

In a single second I vibrate a hundred thousand times.
I want to live the life of Teresa
and let my sacred hand slip
through my scapular.

I want to take the in-no-way-holy path
of Ida Rubenstein,
undressing my body among men
to fill them with a different creed.
At times Curie fills my joy;
other times Duse,
the Poet's beloved who discovers
a glittering rhythm in every voice.
At times I've dreamed of being Princess
Maria of Romania.

At times, not a few times, a peasant
to know only the offices
given to her:

grind tortillas on the metate
singing a song.
I change like a rough wave,
change like the wave
of fire the logs nourish
and which, from far off on a dark night,
glimmers like gemstones.
My soul is a wheel spinning

a hundred thousand times an hour.
And today I am so tired of this world,
of seeing it as it is.

My God, turn the sun blue
and the sky white;
turn the mountains to glass;
the forests red,
stop the human chatter
and let the trees speak
their sadness silenced for centuries;
there must be so much gold in the trees'
secret words.

And God, change me too. I want to be a dryad!
Or a naiad, or a nereid, whatever you want;
I'm tired of human life,
I want to be in touch with the intimate
pure source of all these things;
turn the world inside out
as if it were

a snow-white shirt...
a shirt created by the seamstress.

No, God, I'm already tired of the same old thing.

I know you're a gentleman,
that you listen to the prayers and tears
of a poor woman;
men are too cultured for them.

God, sweet God, you've got me on my knees,
my body between your legs,
my hands on your thighs,
slipping a warm caress
my mouth trembling with prayer,
my eyes on your eyes.

Change this, Lord; but then:
let the sun be blue,
the forest aflame
and make me a nereid.

ÁLVARO FAUSTO TARUMA

Translated by Grant Azevedo Beleza-Schutzman
from Portuguese

The primary challenge I encountered when translating Álvaro Fausto
Taruma's 'Father' was recreating the current that underlies Taruma's
poem. Despite the occasionally unconventional word order of the
original, there is a very natural feel to the poem. I tried to turn each
phrase around until the words found that same rhythm of the
original prose. For example, I found myself trying out a variety
of less direct possibilities when translating the rather simple phrase
'não nos constrange', before finally settling on the version here –
'it's not a bother'.

'Father' reappropriates the image of the night as a sort of 'warm
embrace' to reflect the relation between the narrator and the father.
Language becomes a thread that traverses the barrier between death
and life; it 'glimmers' as starlight and weaves through the waking
dream that the poem evokes with its almost hallucinogenic imagery.
Reading Taruma's prose poetry can sometimes feel like following
a river from end to end; images bleed into another, merging and
separating until finally leading to a conclusion that appears both
inevitable and unexpected.

'Father' moves carefully but quickly, each image fitting with the
others like a puzzle of broken words. In this eulogy for a father, love,
poetry, and language are all bound together inextricably. Translating
it is not a question of just transporting words but of conveying the
connections between these interrelated themes. I've tried to evoke
Taruma's hopeful assertion in a new idiom: no matter the time
that passes, there are things that 'resist forgetting'.

Opposite: Álvaro Fausto Taruma

Father

What amazes me about the night is how at a certain moment the liquid of darkness becomes one with time, one with mud, one with all matter visible and invisible. I begin to suspect that I'm asleep at the very moment you come in. I call out your name just as I could simply call you father, the very word I have not uttered for a quarter-century, but you arrive and the words glimmer and with them the names of the sons that persist below the vastness of the earth. Beneath this pale light we embrace, even though I know I'm asleep and as soon as I wake the horizon will bend into black like every other day; we are not upset that you've opened the book of the dead's weighty page (it's not your fault), on the contrary, we try to laugh because we no longer know where to find tears and we're amazed by the flesh intact at the centre of this rotten world. Sharp as always, you never tell me I'm dreaming nor tell me those old bedtime stories, you stare steadily at the stars – the ones we've come to know – and we go down the long list of names of those who drowned in the September winds, those whose fear guns efface and we toast our tribe and those whose steps we follow across the earth, across the seas, across town squares, across entire cities. We come back to the same libraries where we learned the language of love, with the same lights I will die beneath and that will follow your grandchildren whose improbable manuscripts will speak only of poetry. What amazes me about the night is when I awake from its deceit and realise how your face resists forgetting.

Inventory

Among what is left of memory, there remain countless electric lights, trembling like a mother's hair; pilgrim brooms crisscrossing the courtyard of memories and the house opening itself up to spellbound caves of abandon. Closed up in himself, a father sleeps his final sleep as if after he could escape his death and surprise the morning with blackberries still wet with dew or croon 'blues before sunrise' as fervently as when we sang it on that funereal August afternoon.

A brief wind breaks against the rafters and slowly pushes the thin red sun like children's balloons fashioned counterclockwise in hotel rooms measured by timers and paid for by ancient tales. The parade of stars moves forward through the hissing night across roofs with imprudent cowboys ready to fire on sleep and untangle the voice that proclaims its distant childhood. Women, fresh like certain trees, we climbed until the fruit was bloodied and naked in the rain we remained to feel on our skin its joyful drops and, exhausted but happy, we returned to the widows' feverish laps: hushed birds in their secret nests. Here is the smallest item in this unfortunate sailor's inventory as he revisits the maps of loneliness.

ROXANA CRISÓLOGO

Translated by Kim Jensen and Judith Santopietro from Spanish

Roxana Crisólogo's book *Kauneus: la belleza* (Kaneus: Beauty) is a
distinguished collection of formally innovative poems that give voice
to the alienation and ironies of exile and migration within a leftist
framework embedded in the global struggle against structural
inequality. Set in Peru, Finland, and other regions from Mozambique
to Palestine to Turkey, the poems offer a transnational,
intergenerational feminist poetics irrigated from the vein of
20th century's defeats.

The challenging yet beautiful sequences in *Kauneus* delve into her
family's experience of internal displacement, replicated across Peru,
which has seen waves of migrants leaving rural communities in search
of opportunities in Lima. Crisólogo brings this diasporic sensibility
as she writes about other 'forced countries' and the refugees who flee
poverty, violence, and climate catastrophe.

One of the challenges of translating these poems is the swift
thematic upheavals, ever-shifting subjectivities, and rhetorical leaps
that mark her style. The poems are multivalent and invite a synaptic,
intuitive reading; many seemingly unrelated strands coalesce into
a mosaic that is both figurative and abstract. Having studied law,
Crisólogo deploys and then subverts an ironic form of 'legalese',
drawing attention to the illogic that undergirds the dichotomies
between the global north and south.

As translators we have spent time and care in rendering the
complexities and lyrical dexterity of this poem with its hallucinatory
glimpses into the refractive hall of mirrors created by the social
pressures of inherently discriminatory feminine ideal, objectification,
Orientalism, and the inevitable horizontal hostility among the
marginalised women 'who weren't invited' to the ceremony.

Here we pay homage to Peruvian beauty

The women who weren't invited follow the ceremony
glued to their phones

I get overwhelmed by these kinds of invitations
I don't know which part of me will be cut off by a scalpel
until I'm left wide open   a tumour in the brain
I'm starting to worry about the lines around my eyes
the bags of wasted years
the traces of alcohol that form tinted
fumes when I dream
that make me look too smart too wise
the long dishevelled hair that hangs from me
like a stampede no one ever heard
but a hand appears
and this wasn't in the script   reaches up to arrange it

It seems as though I smile all the time and that's fine
[something flares up on my tongue]
It's better if we correct your position
and your hand falls into place
What if we submerge ourselves like in an aquarium
with little diamond-coloured fish
The relationship of fish to water is unobjectionable
they say yes to everything
and the water laps on and on

What if I say yes to everything and drown myself in tears
A good and sweet mother
forgets about herself

that hand does not forget me
it drives
the anxiety of a hundred eyes waiting for something to happen
It would better if this and everything else could take the shape of
aquarium panes
the winding curves of the things that can't be said

A good wife doesn't drown herself   says the hand
a real woman whom the same hand arranges
to leave her stranded in the centre
of the runway
is the imitation
of another good woman

And I remain lodged like a tumour in everyone's brain
the anxiety of a hundred eyes waiting for something to happen

It seems that none of this is true

a busy bustling avenue
where a man passes   dragging a woman
by her hair

It seems that I'm beautiful
It seems that a downpour of stars will surround my head
It seems that something will explode in front of their eyes

ERIK SOLVANGER

Translated by Astrid Alben from Dutch

Erik Solvanger and I met in 2003 at a poetry event in Perdu, an Amsterdam poetry venue and bookshop. His debut collection, *Simple Trepanations* (De Sandwich-reeks, 2004) was about to come out. Erik was studying to be a GP but switched to psychiatry; I was a writer-in-residence at the Rijksakademie, where I founded the art and sciences initiative PARS. We lived at only a short bike ride from each other and in the summer we would take an end-of-day dive in the river behind where I lived, dry off on the jetty while watching the barges go by, swill cider from a bottle, talk poetry, feet swirling the water's surface – time stretching. Erik left to work as a doctor for Doctors Without Borders in Ethiopia and as a psychiatrist in Tanzania. He inherited the family farm in Zeeland. I moved to London at the time of my debut collection. It wasn't until last year, when Erik invited me to read at the launch of his most recent collection, *Waarom het leven in een witte jas sneller gaat* (*Why Life in a White Coat Moves Faster,* PoëzieCentrum, 2023) that I started translating the poems from that collection now published here. In my experience, a collegial friendship can emerge from the translation process; here, however, the translation came out of a friendship. This doesn't, of course, change the nature of the poems, which, at their core are grotesque and gruesome, absurdist and dark, which is to say, vital and humanistic – and this is what makes Solvanger's poems intriguing.

On the outside she's a floppy doll, we push her
into the narrow tunnel, take pictures of her tiny head.

Images full of motion artefacts, she's afraid
that this will be her tomb, the woman who gave birth to me.

We sing songs to comfort her, a smokescreen
for the trap we meticulously prepared.

I'm sorry, it took some effort but I have found someone
prepared to collect you and who wants to melt you down

into a statue of an animal belonging to a wiped-out race
that existed quite a long time ago, which is far more interesting.

That way, I'll be able to read about you in books penned
by people who completed their PhDs on extinct animals.

After much navigational artistry and luck, I find you again,
an ice-cold clump of cells detached from the perfused mucosa.

Better melt you down first, and only then ask what
do you think of the result, is it better than who you were?

It looks as if someone has taken a small cup
of warm milk and poured it into my skull.

The tissue is soft and viscous,
I have half disappeared.

The scan does not explain
why I started babbling neologisms,

why I wore dresses in the winter
and left trousers flapping in the garden like scarecrows.

Is someone singing a song? How many more nights of sleep
before something like this clears up, before I'm me again?

What white angel has kidnapped me, who took a stick
and beat me lame, my face contorted like that of a clown?

Every night you circle in circles round my house,
watch me roam through my own house like a ghost,

watch my shadow wander from room to room,
until I am gummed to the window like a brown slug.

I gather up the lumps in my throat, scrape
away my dead skin, moisten my lips
and wait — crabs come scuttling through
the mist out of the invisible sea, the distant
lapping of the early mornings, when the sun
still clenches the half moon with its blond pelvis.
The crabs scuttle into my bed pinching their
claws, targeting my hair, my fingers,
my hands, ears, mouth and eyes.
They hide in my skull, lay eggs,
mate in places filled with memories and pain.
Crabs are stunning, their flesh soft pink,
their sweet revenge for the broiled
dream of my parents — this story without end.

DOROTHEA GRÜNZWEIG

Translated by Derk Wynand from German

'Wundbett' or 'Schweissbett' (wound or sweat-bed) is a euphemism
in 'Jägersprache' (hunters' jargon) for the lair in which the bloodied
animal lies.

In an elaborate sustained metaphor in an essay in her selected
poems, *Sonnenorgeln* (Solar Organs, 2011), Grünzweig likens the
creative process to the aurora borealis, the 'foxfire' in the sky or
heaven-sent foxfire that results when radiation from solar flares
collides with the earth's ionosphere. (The German *Himmel* means
both 'heaven' and 'sky'). Her poems often incorporate snatches of
hymns, songs or free-form prayer much heard in the Pietist manse
in which she grew up. '*Ein rein sanft bettelein,*' the final italicised line
of 'wound bed...', is from Martin Luther's 1534 hymn, '*Vom Himmel
hoch, da komm ich her*' ('From Heaven Above to Earth I Come'). For
the Finno-Ugrian Mansi, an indigenous people, some of whose
unique songs Grünzweig translated not long after she moved to
Finland, the bear too is a sacred, 'heaven-sent' animal that comes
from and returns to the sky. The guilt of killing the venerated animal
because it menaces humans and cattle gave rise to extensive rituals
and shaman's songs.

In an essay she recently wrote for her congregation in Helsinki,
'All You Need Is Love', Grünzweig makes a case for biocentric ethics,
leaning away from man's dominion over creation mentioned in
Genesis and toward the more compassionate stances of Noah,
St. Francis and Albert Schweizer. In her latest book *Plötzlich alles da*
(All there in a flash), from which this poem is taken, '*the pietà of
poetry*' (piety, pity, compassion) serves as *ars poetica*. Here it captures
the reverence with which the poet approaches the wounded shebear.
By placing her in the same 'cradle' or 'manger', she heightens the
radical difference in value of the 'worthy' hunter and 'worthless' bear.

wound bed in the veteli woods[1]

it is after all what humans and animals have in common
in which they're a perfect match   the will to live
               and the bitter dying
here they lie together on a layer of moss
wilted leaves in the weteli woods   shebear and hunter
                   converging
the bear riddled by bullets   defending herself
the hunter mauled   here they lie   look
          in mythical twosomeness   if seen from afar
both still alive   clinging to life   their breathing laboured
eyes closed they smell bear moss bog myrtle
            pine needles raining down on them
they hear the wind whisking the birches and
rowan trees   paired listening   paired affliction
             blood seeps into the wound bed
huntsmen call it sweat instead   the hunter feels confident
he'll be rescued   that god wishes him well
          the shebear has no idea what confidence is
now and then sighs burst from her as if she were
an accordion someone carelessly dropped   images
            run through her mind
she is stuck inside her burning body   it slowly founders
        in a lake without foothold   her legs no longer
              want to swim for her
she sees bouquets of ants   honeycombs   ears of corn

---

1 'Wundbett' is a euphemism in the so-called 'Jägersprache' (hunters' jargon)
denoting the place where an animal wounded by a hunter lies.

Opposite: Dorothea Grünzweig

huckleberries   an exposed elk   senses maternal lairs
                her young burrowed into the fur
in a wound bed they lie   where the hunter's hope
is soon rewarded   he hears human voices sees
                men with a stretcher   he'll be carried home

and now their paths diverge   man and shebear are
sundered   just when the bear dashes against
        the lake bottom her images smash into a splintered black

later the bed will be greenwashed by rain   it
works wonders in the wound bed   as though it had never been
anything but   just a cooling concavity in the veteli woods
                        just a cradle a bed soft undefiled

OSIP MANDELSTAM

Translated by Tony Brinkley from Russian

Osip Mandelstam's *Conversation about Dante* can also be read as
a guide to his translators: what is *poetic speech* and how does it
guide translation?

> Poetic speech is a hybrid process which crosses two modes
> of sound: the first of its modes is change (изменение,
> transformation] we hear... motion in its impulse [порыв]... the
> second is speech itself [собственно речь] . . . Poetic speech [is]...
> the merging of these two modes, of which one, considered by
> itself, is completely mute, while the other, abstracted from
> instrumental metamorphosis, is devoid of any significance and
> interest, and lends itself to paraphrase, which to my mind, is the
> surest sign of the absence of poetry: for where a thing is amenable
> to paraphrase, there the sheets have never been wrinkled and
> poetry has not spent the night.[2]

It is the impulse (порыв, which Elena Glazov-Corrigan also
translates as *pneuma,* spirit, 'the vibration of a wave, a change, a
modulation, inaudible on its own, understood only in its effect')
that turns words and phrases into poetry.

Marina Tsvetaeva writes that her poems are not Russian, only
written *in* Russian. In translating a poem from Russian into English,
the translator might discover that the impulse that turns Russian into
poetry also turns the English counterpart into poetry. The translator
translates the impulse – and the words as faithfully as possible – but
only the порыв wrinkles the sheets.

2 Mandelstam, Osip. 1979. Complete Critical Prose. Edited by Jane Gray
Harris and translated by Harris and Constance Link (Ardis: Ann Arbor, 1979)
p.397. Translation modified by the translator.

I am listening—listening to the early ice
That stirs beneath the bridges—
I recall how bright intoxications swim,
Drifting lightly overhead.

From calloused steps, from city squares,
From angled courts—the awkward palaces—
With greater force through satiated lips,
Circling his Florence,
Alighieri chanted.

And here my shadow gnaws the granite
With my eyes, they gnaw the grain—
The rows of logs they see at night
Appear by day to be our homes.

Or else the shadow idles,
Yawns for me,

Or stirs among the servants—
Warmed by heaven, heated by the wine,

And feeds insistent swans
The bitter crumbs...

In the lake water of a rose window, I saw
Fish playing in the facets as they wheeled
Above me—building unleavened dwellings—
While the fox and lion wrestled on the surface
        in a handmade vessel.

Illness gazes inward through the baying dog-
mouthed portals—enemies of closed arches—
The gazelle jumps a violet stairwell and the
Crag-faced tower's pauses. A deep breath.

Centring this town of cricket-artisans—
Rising—a moistening sheath of candid
Sandstone—an ocean boy who rises from
The sweet, unleavened river and tosses cups
        of water at the clouds.
And it was here in heaven that I lost my way—
        what could I do?—you
Who are dear to heaven, will you tell me!
Dante's nine circles—each an athlete's discus:
But it was easier in the past for you to chime.

Do not part me from existence: these dreams
        come to life—
Dreams of killing and, just now, caressing—
So that in my ears, my eyes, their sockets
Lives a Tuscan anguish.

And do not press the sharp,
Caressing laurels on my brow—
Better to cut my heart in fragments—
Into morsels of blue sound.

And when I fall asleep, having served this
        sentence—
A friend of life, a friend of all the living—
Heaven will answer—deeper, higher—
Sounding in my chest while this grows colder.

JEAN D'AMÉRIQUE

Translated by Aidan Rooney from French

When I first listened to Jean D'Amérique's 'Oiseau Blessé' (2023), it stuck in my craw, in a good way. Not translating it was impossible, and I tinkered with it obsessively, trying to catch and near-match its entrancing lyricisms. Already familiar with D'Amérique's writing, I had started watching his performances on YouTube. I still do. Author of four poetry collections, three plays and a novel, his voice sounds an urgent appeal to the francophone world to hear the plight of his native country, Haiti, a country whose people and literature already had a hold on me.

D'Amérique's first novel, *Soleil à Coudre* (Actes Sud, 2021), winner of the 2022 Montluc Resistance and Freedom Prize – opens as follows: 'The birds are crazy above my head, their wings an archipelago of fire'. The bird, an archetype of freedom, is a leitmotif in D'Amérique's work. In a 2021 interview for *Africultures*, he remarked how 'tightening borders and home-confinement, among other repressions... clip our wings, break the élans of our lives'.

In 'Oiseau Blessé', D'Amérique chimes that trope of the wounded bird with the personal despair of the narrator. Here, as in so much of his award-winning work in theatre and poetry, and now more frequently in spoken word and song, beauty and brutality coincide just as frequently as desire and disgust, idealism and realism. He is a voice to be reckoned with and heard.

Overleaf: Jean D'Amérique, photo © Edouard Caupeil

Wounded Bird

Forget poetry.
I get myself a machete
and throw away the roses.
Cradling a trigger,
I fire up on dust
and cut through the prose.
I sell my flesh to scissors,
heart in the embers,
and give back to the blades
what belongs to the wound.
Life lends a hand
but nothingness cuffs me.
Hey, I wanted light
but all that glisters is worth moola.
Me, I go to my abyss.
Say hi to the sun for me.

A bird, a bird,
I am a wounded bird,
wings on a wire fence
hung on barbs of silence.
I am a wounded bird.

Paris overcast is magic for the rich.
Even at high noon my face is full of night.
Let me stroke my silence in the dark.
The song is broken.
I am the son of Alejandra Pizarnik.
Wisdom comes with age

but my youth needs its folly,
let me colour my black thoughts
with a hit of Molly.
The storm gathers.
Soon I will turn the page,
a being broken into tears,
and tear up the flag of my star.

A bird, a bird,
I am a wounded bird,
wings on a wire fence
hung on barbs of silence.
I am a wounded bird.

SAKTHI JOTHI

Translated by Thila Varghese from Tamil

In her poem, 'Liberation', Sakthi Jothi draws a contrast between a
bird that is free to fly anywhere and a woman who remains bound
to her 'cage'.

Watching the seasons change as 'the sprawling neem tree in front
of her house (…) | starts to fill its limbs with blooming flowers' and
the parrots take off from the branches, the woman in the poem recalls
a time when a parrot chick had fallen off a tree branch. The woman
had picked up the little bird with 'a broken beak and injuries to its
body' and cared for it in a cage. Later, when the neem flowers turned
into ripe fruits and the season changed again, she opened the cage
and let the healed bird fly away, as she looked back at 'the house she
could never leave'.

Juxtaposing the situations that the bird and the woman find
themselves in, Jothi argues that a caged bird could fly away when
set free whereas a woman would never be able to follow suit. The
metaphor of the 'caged bird' brings home the point that women,
due to their roles as caregivers and nurturers, are always caught in
a bind, preventing them from 'flying away'. Unlike a bird that is
fundamentally free, a woman is bound by demands and priorities.
Even if she manages to step out of one 'cage', she will inevitably find
herself in another. Seasons may may come and go, but a woman will
always be behind the invisible bars of a cage and thus will never ever
be free as a bird.

Liberation

In the season
of the bare neem tree
in front of the house
filling its limbs
with blooming flowers,
the flocks of parrots taking off
ruffling the top branches
in their hasty flight
still brings back memories
of that day.

One fine morning,
along with the mature leaves,
a parrot fledgling slipped
and fell to the ground.

She scooped up
the little bird
suffering, failing to fly,
with a broken beak
and wounds on the body,
having hurt itself
on the same branch
that it failed to grasp.
She brought it home,
nursed the wounds,
and cared for it
in a little cage.

At the beginning
of the new season
when the flowers on the neem tree
matured and yielded ripe fruits
that filled the place with a bright aroma,
she opened the cage,
and looked back
at the house
she could never leave.

VASYL STUS

Translated by Bohdan Tokarskyi and Nina Murray
from Ukrainian

A psychologically multilayered and lyrically elaborate text, 'Streams'
is one of Vasyl Stus's key poems from the 1960s. The poem charts
Stus' own journey from his childhood as an 'Atlas of slag heaps and
wheelbarrows' collecting coal in Donetsk to his struggle as a
Ukrainian dissident in the Soviet 'forbidden world'. One of Stus's
longest poems (comprising nearly 250 lines), 'Streams' follows not so
much a clearly defined plot as the poetic subject's memories, at times
indeed resembling a stream of consciousness. What unites the
different fragments of the poem (and of the poetic self) is the set of
threads that run through the text, particularly the theme of
childhood. The selected excerpt represents Stus's complex treatment
of this theme. On the one hand, the speaker describes his early years
in moving, synesthetic images such as the tight berries of bells.
On the other hand, a sense of foreboding seeps through his early
memories: the sight of red apples proleptically evokes the smell of
blood. Biographically, this abrupt transition seems to reflect Stus's
growing up during the Second World War and the post-war privation.
That the speaker evokes his mother – the central figure and addressee
in the poem – emphasises his feeling of reverence and guilt towards
her for the hardship she had to endure. Fundamentally, Stus reveals
the tension between the innocent, luminous joy of childhood and the
reality of the human condition with the consciousness of one's
finitude and the vision of childhood as a paradise lost.

from 'Streams'

... it was the real age of exploration,
the day unrolled—a magic carpet:
the world then dawned for me, a little child,
with all its blessings,
and as I took my very first
steps, so I became twofold, threefold.
The suns—a hundred
lustrous bees—then swarmed, and
the stars—the children's scattered
marbles—hung in the sky.
Hands bloomed like flowers,
and the heart's petals quivered
at the sight of home.

And our warm
mining village was my primer—
I hold its letters dear to this day.
Before my eyes I see my happy mother—
she holds my hand and leads me past the orchards
where apples (the red ones, *tsyhanký*) fall to the ground,
their dull thumps resounding through the quiet.
I wonder why, back then, they always used to give me
those scarlet apples? So that I would know
the smell of earth and also human blood?
That's how the ripe sunflowers also smelled, and
the bees as well, and that is how the tears smelled.

And all night long—
there's not a wink of sleep.
And all night long
a mournful ghost, she would
keep standing, beside my bed, in silence
and put her warm, hard
fingers on my forehead
so that I wouldn't
fall asleep,
so that I simply couldn't.
She'd fade away at daybreak.

Behind the wall—a crying child, and someone's laughter
behind the wall. And where to go? And what to do
with those sleepless nights? Behind the wall—two grimaces
nailed into the wall, a pair of wings meant for the blissful after—
both tears and laughter, both behind the wall, both tears and
laughter.

The rain won't stop. It rained through sleep,
all through the night, through dawn.
The gutters sobbed. Or was it all
a mother's long, prophetic weeping?
The daybreak spreads across the sky,
the wistful fog lifts up its feeble
wings. But cannot spread them.
And it's a mortal, deadly sin
to trespass into the dark forbidden—
at will, unchallenged, unimpeded.
The flurry of forgetful snow
comes galloping on its quick feet.

GUNNAR

Translated by Klein Voorhees from German

When 'Threat' was originally published in 1963, sexual relationships between members of the same sex were still illegal in Austria and East and West Germany. Legal recognition of partnerships wouldn't come until the 21st century. The time in which Gunnar lived and wrote was undoubtedly dangerous for LGBTQ+ individuals, but it was not without joy; in spite of legal and social oppression, communities carved out a space in which to unite and support one another. 'Threat' speaks to this unflinching resilience, the belief that though you may be in hiding today, time will march on; 'Nun erschrick', ('Now jump up' or 'Now startle') because spring will come again, and in that time of rebirth will emerge countless opportunities for change. In an era where the rights of our community members are increasingly under fire, I look to voices like Gunnar, to people who stood fast in the face of imprisonment and systemic violence and worked toward a future that was not guaranteed, fueled by the strength of solidarity.

Threat

Beneath the pendulous gait
slumber paradises
of melancholy:
sunken summers.
In their meadows bloom
midnight poppies.
Your clouds wander
along the dark sky
deep beneath the ground,
your shadow world.
Now look alive:
there will be leaves again,
in the reeling of the sun.
You will bloom
in the land of the poppy.
Under its sky
it will strike you,
deadly and unbidden:
bliss.

CEVAHIR BEDEL

Translated by Jeffrey Kahrs and Mete Özel from Turkish

'Cevahir' means jewelry in Turkish and is a nom de plume that has in time come to be the author's name. She took the name on as she associates herself with Edip Cansever, one of the leading Turkish poets of the Second New Movement which began in the 1950s. Technically, Cansever worked in the business of precious metal and stones in the Covered Bazaar in Istanbul, but mostly spent all of his time writing or wandering around his beloved city.

Bedel's style and vocabulary also reflect the 'Ashik' tradition in Turkish poetry. 'Ashiks' were the traditional troubadours of Anatolia who roamed from village to village playing and singing songs based on the stories and myths that were current at the time. Her Turkish reflects this influence as the language is simple but forceful. The rhythm of her poems, at first glance, seems to consist of highly structured lines. But her language isn't structured, at least not in a traditional sense. She maintains the musical flow of words from the older traditions. As Bedel says, her poetry is 'processed from raw matter into a more refined form by bumping into other poems, lives, and people over time'.

Bedel is from a minority community called the 'Alevi', who tend to be more open to the changing times. Perhaps this is why in her writing, rather than focusing on a very specific time and place, Cevahir tends towards considering universal concerns. In these elegies she is very much considering the effects of evil.

first elegy

the squalid word dresses itself
in evil rooms as hands wash in filth
harvesting truth
believe me everything breaks believe me

houses are emptied balconies yellowed
by cigarette smoke entering sneezing corridors
waves move across streets
to meet shores beyond the sea

suddenly forgetting we suddenly forget
but what unconsciously keeps us together
is a pile of sparrows and unscented funeral flowers

remember
we collected *kenger*[3]
and only i returned
what was that sour taste in my mouth

who killed/i killed
who washed/i washed
who buried/i buried...

3 *Gundelia tournefortii, an endemic, edible plant.*

second elegy

taking a shower in scorching heat
a cool splash is a slash across the skin
a name blooms there for just a day

taking a long walk we soon
became hungry in a green meadow
touched by eternity a red tree
a place without time

sitting at the base of a rock
watching the lake and boats passing through us
we didn't feel cold for the first time
because pain wrapped around us like a blanket

do you recall we explored towns
forgetting we are made of water we asked
for fire from women carrying
sunlight in their mouths

whoever died/i died
whoever's been washed/i've been washed
whoever's buried/i've been buried

third elegy

i wouldn't come if you didn't invite me
half a body half a mind half a portion of pain
i was a narrow street running into you
here and there

coming and going to your table
i was about to have a snack there
when birds in the sky appeared
flock of wings i carried on my back

i was kept waiting in a wide courtyard
with cool stones... how pleasing
to welcome the evening with you
were children singing? i felt warm

if you hadn't told me i couldn't recall
who i was: a small space, a breeze,
a moment posing in a photograph
don't remind me, save me...

who died/i died
who was washed/i was washed
who was buried/i was buried

YOUR LANGUAGE ANTICIPATING MINE

Focus on Catalan

GEMMA GORGA

Translated by Sharon Dolin from Catalan

These poems from *Voyage to the Centre* (*Viatge al centre*, 2020), Gemma Gorga's most recent poetry book, are extreme acts of compression that work through diminution and subtraction. She explores how poems consisting of very few words can convey meaning. Gorga understands both the power and the limits of language; these poems occupy the liminal space between speech and silence. Using a minimalist style, Gorga has written limpid poems that rely on image and metaphor. They are also meditations on the process of poetic creation.

Three in the Morning

Maybe get up
open the fridge
collide with the whale's eye
that makes the tiles glow
with its arctic blue
devour anything
let anything devour you
look at the lightwell over there—
                    false hope
                    of a twin soul—
have your doubts about a pill
write four lines
pretend it's a poem
that tomorrow will be
nothing of the kind.

At Water's Edge, Mary Shelley Is Inspired

I like this pink, slightly rough
stone. It reminds me
of a weary heart—
as mine is now, as never
before.

I'm keeping it warm in my hand,
incubating it with utter tenderness.

Insects and stars pause mid-flight:
                                        listening.

The stone is beginning to beat
and open its eyes
inside my fist's brutal dark.

ÀXEL SANJOSÉ

Translated by Richard Dove from Catalan

The two Àxel Sanjosé poems presented here engage mutually related opposites: past vs. present/reality vs. imagination. 'Rearguard' develops a notion of life as a sort of (forced) march, during which the inner and outer world are both devastated, whereas the realm of the frogs – at once enigmatic and trivial – remains invisible and thus safe.

In 'Time, they say...' the subject, again a collective narrator, does not move. The all-changing dynamic of time is shifted outwards and reduced to a visual illusion. Characteristically, a sign's presence (seagulls, frogs) triggers the same interpretation as its absence, demonstrating its obsoleteness. Although the sea, gulls and rosemary – and even the sedge and frogs – may be reminiscent of the Catalonian landscape in which Sanjosé grew up, his poetry is markedly non-biographical. The setting, far from picturesque, is decidedly abstract – and could be perceived as symbolistic, were it not for the insistent questioning of symbols and tokens of any kind undergirding the poet's work.

Sanjosé's deep scepticism towards language (a sign system, after all), inherited from German hermeticist Günter Eich, appears to coalesce with the labyrinthine, death-focused allegorical world of Catalonia's major poet Salvador Espriu.

Perhaps ambiguity is an overriding trait: at the end of 'Rearguard', Hölderlin's idealistic asseveration 'What remains, though, poets create' is twisted through a Celanian grinder ('No one bears witness for the witness'). In 'Time, they say...', 'serenity' emerges, quite possibly, on the other side of despair as a species of agnostic faith.

Rearguard

On past the granary, on past the manor,
don't tremble, don't glance now,
our elderly tools slung over our shoulders.

On past the willows,
the age-old and tardy avenue,
on past the pond, on past, on past
the hideaways from when we were children.
Singing: dust clings to the palate.

The pond there is acroak with frogs
(don't tremble, don't glance now),
the sun's stretching out among the sedge,
we cleave, used to cleave, have cleaved.

No testimony: that's what remains.
They're now croaking louder, with greater beauty,
we never once glimpsed them.

Time, they say...

but it's just
the light that's changing.

Once we saw gulls:
we imagined the sea.
Once no gull:
we imagined the sea.

Serenity
is time's
contrary.

Treat this as if it were
fresh rosemary.

ANNA GUAL

Translated by AKaiser from Catalan

Anna Gual is a prolific prize-winning Catalan poet and author of eight collections of poetry. She is a mainstay in the European literary world, with collections also translated into French, Italian and Spanish. From her first book, *Implosions* (2008), now in its fourth edition, to her most recent, *Les ocultacions* (Proa, 2022), winner of the Miquel de Palol Prize, Gual has demonstrated a talent for expressing life in all its unexpectedness, whether she is exploring – excavating if need be – relationships among human beings and the rest of our universe, between and within bodies, or in the flesh and blood of language itself. Think Vievee Francis, think Ingeborg Bachmann, think Samuel Beckett. Poets such as Lluís Calvo consider Gual's work 'a territory of continuous exceptionalities'; Susanna Rafart remarks that to enter Gual's work is to enter a 'forest of wild rebirths'; Gemma Gorga describes Gual's poetic world as one where 'human laws are far away.'

'Re-re-re-besàvia' / 'Great-great-great great grandmother' is from *Altres semideus* (LaBreu Edicions, Barcelona, 2019) and is also included in *Unnamable*.

'La petició' / 'The petition' is from *Les Ocultacions* (Editorial Proa, Barcelona, 2022, 3rd Edition), winner of the Miquel de Palol Prize, and the work I am currently translating, *Hidden Things* (working title).

Great-great-great great grandmother

The right to surrender is not a right,
you should tell someone who resembled me.
It's a semantic error.
It's a magma hoax.

All centuries are the same century.
Only the colours and shapes change.

The customs.
The bacteria.

You have always inhabited all times.
You have always lived within me.
Alive and dead, at the same time.

Urged on by those who push,
barefoot,
a carriage.

The Petition

Light up the face of the stone,
the inner part of the shell,
the hidden hemisphere of the eye.

Let shine all
that has mass and occupies volume
but which you cannot detect
with the retina.

Bring the flashlight closer
to what escapes optical range,
what ignites the contradiction
of having eyes and not seeing.

Clarify what emits photons
to which our pupils are not sensitive.

Let me see
the birth of the stars,
the expansion of the universe,
your language anticipating mine.

Enlighten me
of what I will never see.

JOSEP CHECA

Translated by Ronald Puppo from Catalan

Josep Checa (Caldes de Montbui, 1962) explores and depicts the power of everyday things in rural and small-town settings like the Catalan countryside where he grew up. Going to work in a textile factory at age sixteen – and attending evening classes to earn his high school degree – shaped his singular perspective on the self and the world, sharpening his ability to query the commonplace and glean the wonder therein. As a counterpoint to his job as a farmer and father of two children, Checa approaches his vocation as both a poet and a literary activist. His wife, Esther Obradors, collaborates as his pre-publication critic and illustrator. On the urgency of the poet's task, Checa writes: 'The configuring of today's world, on the whole, works against poetry, but there are always fissures, and there is a backdrop of emptiness and disquiet that poetry can put right'.
In 'Friday, three in the morning', the poet is summoned by an owl to make a standstill journey through the window opening on to the mysterious natural life outside. The owl's departure, when called away by a second owl in the distance, leaves the poet in a blanket of darkness and silence that drives a wedge between him and the woods where he had once lived and found peace. As poet and critic Àlex Susanna suggests, Checa's poetry reveals a world that is the woods, harbouring an evasive mystery but also a hidden complicity, just out of reach, and yet served up and seen, and felt, through the uncanny triumph of poetry.

Opposite: Josep Checa, photo © Esther Obradors

Friday, three in the morning

The night deep dark, in the small hours
an owl came hooting at the window.
It had rained and the streets echoed the wet.
Farther off, in the foliage of a tree
another hoot rose in reply.
After a brief chat, the owl took wing
flapping in silence the silence of the night.
I recalled having lived in the woods some time ago,
the sounds that had then brought me peace
out by the ancient dreams of tall oaks.
I lay awake waiting for the owls, till daybreak,
or perhaps it was they who waited in the woods.

The Death of Poets

awash in the turbid river of words

could someone read the life on its ceaseless way?

will someone raise the cities of poets
remembering only their verses?

will the word be stone
                              be rain
be damp morning and smell of coffee
and children
                  the square
                              the fountain?

will someone remake the landscape that we wrote?
will the wind comb the hayfields as always
and the sprouts of hope
once more move the earth?

will something akin to happiness
fill certain winter afternoons

with no other certainty than that someone loved someone?

TÒNIA PASSOLA

Translated by Ronald Puppo from Catalan

Tònia Passola wields the subtle power of imagery energised by an adroit command of the wordsmith's craft with a view to transcending the limits of ordinary language, resulting in the creation of an extraordinary poetic world. In her longer journey-poems ('Galta' and 'Mesopotamia'), her poetry gives new life to the journeys where renewal permeates the interface between self and world. To put it another way, poetry is the catalyst that transports us beyond perceived boundaries. Philippe Tancelin has remarked how, in Passola, 'the line of the horizon suddenly comes loose, dislodging from our eyes its preset contours and bringing into view the restful beach of thresholds.' In 'Desire', Passola journeys to the depths of the self in confrontation with the world and, equally, her own self. To clear the hurdles dotting the path to desire's completion, the wisdom to open the way stems from 'hear-tell', that is, from an unspecified source, or to be more exact, from a pool of uplifting popular lore that the poet has tapped into and perhaps strengthened into the bargain. In 2014, Passola was honoured with the Nënë Terezë award in the city of Gjakova in the Republic of Kosovo; in 2015, the Alexander the Great award on the Greek island of Salamis; and in 2017, the Special Award at the International Poetry Festival Ditëtenaimit in Tetovo, North Macedonia.

Desire

I'd heard tell that desire can come knocking
at the door of no-desire,
and that if the latter is shut, makes its entrance inch by inch.
And that it can spin a wondrous web
around no-desire, winding it in the fervent
thread of the eye's gaze.
And that, at times, it is a lightning bolt
that bursts through dark summits.
The rioting rock
that strikes the high-soaring imagination of risk.
The not-quite-right gift
that suddenly warms the heart.
And they told her (today she had a taste of that hear-tell)
that desire will at long last flood
the unruly dry of the most hostile of regions.

SÍLVIA AYMERICH-LEMOS

Translated by Matthew Geden from Catalan

I first encountered the poems of Sílvia Ayermich-Lemos at the Cork World Book Fest back in 2019. Initial translations were developed in a workshop setting and I also attended a reading by the poet herself, getting a sense of her distinctive voice. The original poems are lyrical with a musicality that resounds through the repetition of vowels and alliteration. I was also struck by the range of influences in the work, the poems are contemporary and utterly global in their references as the poet subtly weaves in echoes of other writers into her own texts.

Ayermich-Lemos is concerned with language, clearly evident in the poem 'If the Words Entice Me In', a poem about reading but also writing, a meta-poem in fact. Her interest in language isn't confined to her native Catalan but also to her engagement with multiple languages on different levels and this has resulted in a long-term project, Multiple Versions, a platform for poetry translation that promotes minority languages alongside those more widely spoken.

My own translations therefore are part of an ongoing conversation, my own attempts to read her work. In the process of translation, I'm hoping to find echoes of the poet's own voice in the rhythms and repetitions, a voice that is wry, cosmopolitan and yet also rooted in the rural and urban landscapes of her home in Catalonia.

If The Words Entice Me In

If the words entice me in,
I will unshell them
reveal their ambiguities
written into every line,

I will taste

their crudity on my tongue
the sadness inside
the tender bloom of their draw.

Alnus Glutinosa
(Black Alder)

When the wayward wind cries out
suddenly, withdraws
from your own most secret garden
lovers, babies
even pyres
        of dead leaves,

how can you forgive
the infamous alder
for giving shelter?

Nevertheless,
in the medicine you find hard to swallow,
the bark that soothes sore throats
must surely be desired.

Sadly, Wisława,
I can't tell you anything
you don't already know...

SÍLVIA AYMERICH-LEMOS

Translated by Sílvia Aymerich-Lemos and
Kathleen McNerney from Catalan

Writing in a minoritised language, no matter how many speakers
it has, is a major handicap for any poet. It hinders their chances of
reaching a broader audience. Self-translation is an opportunity to
somehow reverse this unfavourable situation for those proficient in
English and willing to engross themselves in the demanding task of
translating their poems. In short, it is a luxury for the chosen few.

Being brought up as a trilingual student (Catalan, French,
Spanish) at the Lycée Français-Barcelona (3–18 years old),
self-translating my poetry into French had not been beyond my
capabilities. But translating one of my poems into English, as
Dr. McNerney suggested in 2013, was more of a challenge. The fact
that she didn't send corrections on my very first attempt – a stroke
of beginner's luck – built an atmosphere of trust between us. I knew
I could do it as far as I had her, the wisest guide, by my side. She
has a sound background in both languages (English and Catalan),
a broad scope and an amazing capacity to wrestle with my 'creativity'
in English – i.e. not discarding unusual linguistic choices just
because I am not a native speaker or accepting all my suggestions
just because I am the author.

For 'Alghero', in particular, McNerney's improvements included
punctuation (a comma after 'dwellings'); connotations ('eyes half
open' instead of 'eyes ajar' as 'ajar' is associated with doors),
precision ('stroll along' rather than 'go across').

Alghero

To all those Alguerese[4] with a coral heart

On tiptoes, with eyes half open
I stroll along your narrow streets,
your pebbled lanes,
flooded in the salty pervasive smell
of your *marina* – My dearest Mediterranean Sea! –
I'm as used to these old surges as you,
living surrounded by bastions
where the white wave knocks on
insistently,
on behalf of centuries.
You are Sardinian. Even though you're as fond
as I am of your ill-fated tongue,
an island within a parched wild island.

But when that blazing sun
burns the skin of your dwellings,
when Naples pulls out your men's coral heart
and the wind snatches
their seaweed hair...
Your six-hundred years' longing
            deeply stabs at my entrails.

---

4 Even though only 10-15% of the population speak Alguerese Catalan in
the city of Alghero, the inhabitants like to call their city 'Barceloneta',
i.e., 'little Barcelona'.

FELÍCIA FUSTER

Translated by Marialena Carr from Catalan

Though Felícia Fuster (Barcelona, 1921-Paris, 2012) is a poet of tangible objects (household, bodily, geological), her imagery flees from logic and her syntax contorts as it demands the reader's close attention.

This is the second poem of ten within the third and last section (*And more*) of her book *And Yet (I Encara, 1987)*. It begins with the word 'and', creating a conversational tone, further reinforced by addressing a plural you, which is a challenge in an English translation. The 66-year-old poet is defiant in the face of ageing, being silenced by adverbs, and having her memories shut away: she will keep walking, existing, writing, painting.

To translate this poem I tried to go beyond primary definitions to find the echoes of meaning. The central image, a 'volcà antic', is literally an 'old volcano', but what truly matters with volcanoes is their activity. Nevertheless, my first and final choice was 'ageing' because of references to time and physical decline. The rich options of 'extinct', 'inactive', or 'dormant' contradict her claim of an illicit explosion, even if she may (seem to) be reduced to smoke and steam.

Sight permeates the entire poem though most explicitly in the last stanza, where the calendar is 'cec', i.e., blind, but also clogged or blocked, and by eyes. Here I lose the word play in translation. Modigliani often painted eyes entirely in one colour. The poet's eyes might 'glaze over', 'be drowned' or 'heaped with salt' but the poet will go on, even without stars for light.

Overleaf: Felícia Fuster

And more

II
And all of you are worlds.
I,
maybe just an ageing volcano
full of doubts. Maybe the crisscross,
            aimless,
            of a brush flying
            over canvas.
            Or nothing.

I don't know what day it is, what space,
what system. I walk
with dazed bones and legs
wasted by the yellowing,
            by the leaves
            that think themselves birds,
            and I don't ask
            for another sky.

Mine is the illicit explosion,
each day's quick hit or miss,
and the moon cycle opening way
to new alignments
            – clouds of fresh sulphur –
            flecking with rust
            at the flick
            of fingernails.

I look for summer
because hemlines rise

and, yearning, the heart splinters.
In the rounded brightness of public squares
       I erase myself
       and away slips
       that silence
       inside that sinks me.

And what excess is missing from the frame
of the door that closes memory
and weighs it on scales of smoke.
So heavy is the telex
       that writes us
       in bruising insistence
       the dregs
       of adverbs.

And all of you, whole and immanent,
maybe you are still worlds
and you write by quill.
I am almost, of the volcano,
just the steam and smoke. So be it:
if I must go on, I go on. What day
is it? I'll walk through the calendar clogged
by eyes bewildered and empty and filled
with Modigliani green
even if I take a dive and my own
glaze over, if they're drowned,
       if they're heaped
       in salt, if the night
       strips away
       my stars.

JOSEP CARNER

Translated by Niall O'Gallagher from Catalan

Though Josep Carner was just twenty-two when *Els Fruits Saborosos* appeared in 1906, the publication of this slim volume of only eighteen poems was quickly recognised as a turning point for Catalan poetry. The book came to be seen as the foremost expression of a new aesthetic in the Catalan arts, urbane and classical, in which the perfection of Catalan as a literary language would play a defining role. Carner himself described these poems as 'idylls'. Each poem concerns a different fruit – strawberries, oranges, apples, apricots – and presents a scene in the lives of Carner's fictional protagonists. Some – like Pandara in 'Like the Strawberries' – are children; others look back on their youth from the perspective of old age. The figure of the poet himself, whose role it is to transform these everyday occurrences into art, only emerges at the end. Repeatedly revised and republished during the poet's lifetime, Josep Carner seems to have seen *Els Fruits Saborosos*, his third collection, as crucial to his development, placing the sequence at the beginning of his collected volume, *Poesia* (1957), from which the texts translated here are taken.

The first two poems in the sequence are presented here. The rhyme and metre of these English translations echo the form of the Catalan originals. When Josep Carner began writing, Catalan lacked a standard written form, so his poetry uses words from different Catalan dialects and from older literature as well as neologisms he coined himself as he enriches and extends his language.

I. Like the Strawberries

The grandmother feasts on early summer strawberries;
she prefers the freshest fruits, the ones that children find.
And so, her favourite granddaughter Pandara, sweet and young
(everyone knows her, she is enchanted by the light,
growing every day in contentment and delight;
sometimes she lifts her face towards the sky and wanders blind,
that girl whose words are still not bold, who never quips,
her senses all jumbled up in a song)
        now plucks a clutch of tight-packed strawberries
        covered in pink juice to her finger tips.
Each morning she sits sheltered from the wind
        by the strawberry plot;
she sees the breeze cast shadows on the ground
and her body stoops to pick one without thought.
She likes the creeping jenny and the well-kept park
and believes the heavens end just behind the yard.
The strawberry tree is protected in its shady lair,
but God's work is in vain as Pandara seeks her prize;
blushing as she picks the strawberries without a care,
if she finds two together she laughs and lifts her eyes.
Pandara has only ever seen untroubled skies;
she ignores the tempest and the witches' cries.
The full perfect light is life and faith to her.
The world, teeming with miracles and playful pleasures
is small and red and fresh, just like the strawberries.

II. *Aglae and the Oranges*

In the distance, from the shade of a great orange tree
Aglae hears her sisters, like birdsong on the air.
She doesn't chase through dewy grass to join their company
but stays beneath the branches, her face white with despair.

She danced and laughed with Drias, his newly wedded bride,
haughty among the clamour and buoyed up by the light.
But now, among the garden's forgotten paths, she hides
and, lost among its fragrances, grows ever more white.

When she reaches the oranges, Aglae harvests her prize;
at the very sight of them the thirst makes her eyes flare.
She takes a bite and, in ecstasy, closes her eyes,
and, using both her hands, she loosens out her hair.

And Aglae, now remade, is shaken with bliss
her fallen heart rises with a tender sigh
(she could greet the child that now approaches with a kiss),
with a beat so simple yet so unrecognised.

She sees the poor orange that had been so fine
lying abandoned in the ditch, by her mirror's side.
From this woman, all joy and happiness shines,
wrung out and set free by the freshness of a child.

MARIA-MERCÈ MARÇAL

Translated by Clyde Moneyhun from Catalan

Along with her achievements as a poet, essayist, critic and editor, Marçal also is responsible for rediscovering and reprinting Catalan-language women poets whose work was suppressed during the Franco dictatorship (1939–1975). She herself became the most important subsequent link in the chain of 'literary mothers' across the 20th century.

Her poetry ranges from free verse to sonnets, from songs that echo troubadour poetry to the nursery rhymes that Marçal treasured and considered to be the folk music of women and children. Through it all, a consistent voice employs a repeated set of images. From a Catalan literary tradition that extends to the Middle Ages, there are castles and dark forests, swords and shields, bards and heartbroken lovers. From children's tales, there are fairies and witches, magicians and sorcerers, love potions and poisons. The epigraphs of her poems are an index to the major figures of centuries of Catalan literature.

One set of images in particular conveys her profoundly feminist view: the very specific flora and fauna of her poetic world, a world that is explicitly feminine. Even inanimate elements take on animate life, especially the moon. In the still very conservative social climate after the end of the Franco dictatorship in 1975, Marçal courageously explored the theme of lesbian desire in all her work, and also lived an openly lesbian life in long-term relationships with women. Marçal was diagnosed with cancer in 1997 and died in 1998 at the age of 43. Posthumous volumes continue to appear, including collections of poetry, literary criticism, political essays, feminist theory, and diaries and letters.

Clouds with Woodworm

Lily among thistles, an oven within me
bakes a bread loaf of sweetest taste,
that nonetheless gives off a bitter scent.
— Ausiàs March

If we kiss in the streets
the houses will quake.
— Miquel Martí i Pol

Curtains burn
the panes, the anguish.

The chasm of midnight.

Outside, worms
grate the moon.

One o'clock tolls.

Love hangs
strangled from a tree.

The clock has stopped.

*   *   *

Upon a patched-up sky
we set love free at the gray hour:
the headboard reflects our ruin.

Tanit

In vain the showers try to drown the embers
that scorch the clouds. At that moment a girl
passed by with her cheeks painted crimson
and her forehead sparkling. I saw that she had raised
her hands as if to catch some small thing
and then gave up on it.
I see you, now that you speak, Tanit, and you bring to mind
those willows with fierce branches that line the way
to the fields of the Devil—where we went
on bicycles and threaded blackberries
in spears of wheat—, forbidding branches.
I will distance myself from you, Tanit, until your head
is no more than the eye of a needle stuck in a scrap of
gleaming satin;
the mountain will welcome me with embraces of fennel
—while chewing a tender shoot I will forget the way—
and the rain, a corsair with burning coals for eyes,
    will bolt for the east.

GABRIEL FERRATER

Translated by Adrian Nathan West from Catalan

Much ink has been spilled about Gabriel Ferrater in Catalan: about his relationship to language, about the moral qualities of his work (which, I confess, largely elude me), about his relationship to the French moralists of the eighteenth century, to Robert Graves or Robert Frost, to the mediaeval Valencian poet Ausiàs March. To recapitulate that here would offer readers the silhouette but not the substance of understanding. The poem has to stand on its own: this is true of its original and of its translation. I will share here that my method is no method beyond the principle that better is better; that I respect the strictures of rhyme, register, and metre, but will break them prudently for the sake of euphony. As for the poet, when asked what he could say about himself upon the publication of his first book, he offered the following, which is better than anything I could write: 'I was born in Reus in 1922. The remaining events of my life are more uncertain and more difficult to date. I like gin with ice, the paintings of Rembrandt, the ankles of young women, and silence. I detest houses where it's cold inside and ideologies'.

Daybreak

Night that deserts me, one night more, and the wing
of a tremendous fallen plane interposed
between dense blue and window, and I wonder
if it is a feeble green or silver, cold
like the fine insistent scalpel that carves
the uterus with an imposition of excess life,
or light itself when breaking open
the child's hand which tires of struggling
to irritate his siblings, feigning to hide
who knows what precious object, and loses
his prey, and I know nothing will come of it
apart from my disenchantments yesterday,
and it chills me to look at myself another day,
slavered fruit pit peeled and pulped, prone at night.

Idols

Then, when we lay
embracing at the window
open to the slope of olive trees
(two seeds in one fruit split
apart by summer, and filled
with air) we had no memories. We
were the memory we have now. We
were this image. The idols of ourselves
in the submissive faith of afterward.

MARIA ANTÒNIA SALVÀ

Translated by Clyde Moneyhun from Catalan

Salvà stands out among other Catalan-language writers for being not from Catalonia, but rather from the island of Mallorca in the Balearic archipelago that is now part of Spain. Catalan is an official language of the island group (which includes Menorca, Ibiza, and Formentera), and Salvà incorporated elements in her writing of the variation known as *mallorquí*. We see this reflected in her poems, from grammar to idioms to lexicon. Some of her vocabulary is so particular that examples from her poems are used to illustrate many otherwise unknown words in Francesc de Borja Moll´s *Diccionari català-valencià-balear*, the definitive ten-volume dictionary of the language.

Countless Catalan-language poets, particularly women, consider Salvà to be a groundbreaking pioneer for her poetic style and choice of subject matter, as well as for her ability to forge a career in a sphere dominated by men. In a prescient short poem, she imagines how she may be regarded in the future:

To the Young Ladies of the Year 2000

Oh you, foretold flowers of love and kindness
who will live when my footsteps have been erased;
I send to guide you, in friendship, a greeting
from the past, my flock of verses in flight.

She was a prolific translator, notably of Frédéric Mistral, the Nobel Prize winning Provençal poet, and of Italian novelist Alessandro Manzoni. The title of her autobiography, *Entre el record i l'enyorança* (1955), introduces the two great themes of her work: *Between Memory and Longing*.

Opposite: Maria Antònia Salvà

On a Cactus

Like a monstrous reptile with spotted skin,
with slimy entrails, it was settled
in its corner, drinking in the sun.
Suddenly, its malice awakened,
contorting itself, it broke its pot.
Leaving no tracks out of the garden,
it tumbled from the top of a dry stone wall,
and after a while, digging in the cracks
and crevices of the sharp rocks,
I found the old dragon, ferocious still.

The Seashell

Love and its remembrance, which freed me
from people, from time, from place,
populated my life magically
with lovely sparks of silver and gold.
Dusk arrived, melting away the mirages;
I bid them farewell—all things pass away—
and made do, half-hearted,
with a seashell from a distant shore.

MERCÈ RODOREDA

Translated by Rebecca Simpson from Catalan

These two poems come from Mercè Rodoreda's 'World of Ulysses', an 'unfinished though not incomplete' sequence of thirty-two sonnets and songs. Her poetry was only collected in 2002: *AGONIA DE LLUM — La poesia secreta de Mercè Rodoreda* (Angle Editorial, Barcelona).

Several writers turned to the 'Odyssey' as a source text for new work after the devastating wars of the first half of the twentieth century. Mercè Rodoreda was one of the few women to do so. Alongside Odysseus, Agamemnon and the Cyclops, Rodoreda gives voice to female characters: Penelope, Calypso, Anticlea, the Sirens. Rodoreda presents anonymous individuals, too, such as a nameless soldier, a dead girl, the women servants of Ithaca.

'[The Miller Woman's Lament]' follows three 'songs' with a Lorquian cadence, from a group of miller women. I wished to reflect the short, sharp syllables with their plosive Ps, and almost hawking Cs in 'tres cops escupo', meaning 'three times I spit'; given the onomatopoeic monosyllable 'spit', I chose a less literal translation for the final line. The other group of women in 'World of Ulysses' are washerwomen or laundresses who accompany the young Nausicaa. They have two songs: an evocation of dawn and 'Song of The Laundresses, II' which offers images of duality, and of a world 'on the other side'. Many anonymous voices belong to the dead in this remarkable poetry cycle, written as Rodoreda was emerging from both a paralysing writer's block and the trauma of war.

[The Miller Woman's Lament]

My knees are ruined, I'm done in,
and I have to mill three sacks by tomorrow;
the other girls trooped off without me
before the sky was caught in a starry web.

Hands sunk in flour,
my brain—tinier than a grain of wheat—
dreams of a soft bed, clean sheets
and a warm bath to rid me of fine dust.

O crusty bread, wrought gold bar!
What an effort it takes, before the oven
may turn your grey paste golden-brown!

So much dust, so much work is poisoning me,
the summer of the fields dwindles beneath my eyes;
Spit, spit, spit, and no-one will ever know.

Song of The Laundresses, II

Framed in the river's window
we look at ourselves from there within.
O, it's sad to have sisters
in the river, upside down!
With our same colours
and just a bit wavy.

—Perhaps it's the weary water
half imagining us.

When we do the white washing
they all come to rinse
pretend cloths, the false laundry
of those who live in the wet;
and if they can, they pull
our finest sheets away.

—Perhaps we're on one side *and* the other
with water sighing in between.

JOSEP LLUÍS AGUILÓ

Translated by Anna Crowe from Catalan

Josep Lluís Aguiló shares with the great Argentinian writer, Jorge
Luis Borges, a predilection for myths, labyrinths, secret libraries, the
hermetic and the magical. In another poem, 'The Secret Library',
Aguiló pays homage to Borges (the 'blind librarian'), as well as to the
great mediaeval Mallorcan writer, Ramon Llull, whom he pictures
deciphering the pages of the natural world, that 'thicket of writing,
the green and yellow words | of chapters written by a botanical god'.

Aguiló's work has a strong attachment to his own rural and
maritime landscapes in the Balearics, and can be imbued, like Borges'
work, with a touch of 'magic realism'. The poet's first encounter with
the 'Sun Tree' is described in a child's voice, but tantalisingly, and
typically, the poet withholds just what it is the Tree 'just did'. The
second sighting is fleeting and ends in disaster, while the last sighting
(he spies it from his boat, growing on a cliff) brings the realisation
that he must be content with having seen it three times. It is perhaps
significant that it is the child who has the closest encounter, and
Aguiló uses a child's view of the world in other poems to expose or
reveal truths. Each reader will bring their own way of interpreting just
what the Sun Tree may stand for, though perhaps the final message
of the poem is a call to live in the present: a joyful affirmation of the
power of the imagination, of the strangeness of life itself.

The Sun Tree

It is not down on any map; true places never are.
                                        – Hermann Melville

I came across the Tree while we were walking
through a field quite near the school.

We were walking in single file, on an excursion.
I was a child who had just learned to write.

I remember that they had pinned
to my jersey a paper disc, brightly coloured
and with my name on it: a medal.

And when I found the tree in front of me
I turned to my nearest companion
and said to him "Did you see it? Did you see what it did?"

The second time I saw it was when
we were approaching Cordoba on a train.
I was eighteen and on my travels.

As we were coming towards a station,
looking through the window of the carriage,
for a few seconds I saw it, in a square.

In order to try and reach it I leapt
off the train and fractured my left leg.
In plaster, with this marble leg,
following the tracks, for a whole afternoon
I tried, in vain, to find it.

The last time I found it again
was a year ago: we had come by boat
to Formentera, sailing, and we were
happy and tired. Rounding the Cap
de Barbària I was able to gaze at it
for a while. It was growing out of the side
of the cliff, as though trying to keep its balance.

The following day I was on the point of going back there,
overland, but I didn't dare to do it.
At my age nothing takes me by surprise any more
when the stuff of dreams infects my mind.

Each time I've seen it I've said to myself
I don't know whether I'll ever see it again,
and I grow sad but, soon,
I tell myself how lucky I am because
I hold one of the last mysteries of the world.

Without ever searching for it, it has been given to me
to have seen the Sun Tree three times;
one more than the number of times Ahab
found himself face to face with the white whale.

MIQUEL MARTÍ I POL

Translated by Lourdes Manyé and Wayne Cox from Catalan

Miquel Martí i Pol (1929–2003) lived in Roda de Ter (Catalonia,
Spain) and is the most widely-read poet in contemporary Catalan
literature. He collaborated with Joan Miró, and before the onset of
multiple sclerosis, he was a folk singer who wrote lyrics and poetry
that appear in over forty CDs by famous Spanish and Catalan
musicians. He won the Premi d'Honor de les Lletres Catalanes in
1991, the most important literary award in Catalan literature, and in
1992 was awarded Spain's highest literary honor: the Medalla de Oro
al Mérito en las Bellas Artes. In 2000 he was nominated for the
Nobel Prize for literature.

When working on our translation of his 1976 book *Quadern de
vacances* (*Vacation Notebook*), we became friends with him and his
wife Montserrat, and when we published our translation of *Vacation
Notebook* (Lang, 1995) he wrote the preface for us. Since then, we have
presented on Miquel Martí i Pol at conferences, given many readings,
and published translations and articles on him in several well-known
scholarly and literary periodicals.

These three poems come from *Després de tot* (*After all*) (Edicions
Proa, 2002), the last book of poems he published, in which he reflects
on his life, memories and principles as he is getting old. In 'Time
Saved,' memory helps recover a time lived fully; in 'Oasis', he honors
a space in which reflection and conversation take place peacefully;
and in 'Invitation to Dance', the poet affirms his identity at this
stage of his life.

Opposite: Miquel Martí i Pol

Time Saved

Indifference is like a vast inertia
that hides its name and breaks all the rhythm.
I recall the sublime embraces of old,
arousing almost, and above all naïve,
and I recall the tempting evenings spent
by an ocean I only imagined.
Our story is recollection, drawn out
like a long spool of thread we unravel
measuring its meaning with the numb fingers
of memory, trying to recover
movements and intentions from a deep,
unsuspected and fragile stillness.
No time is lost, and in the well of sentiment
water is always renewed, and it revives
the necessary thirst, the great pulse
of desire that puts life to the test.

Oasis

The place is pretty austere but pleasant.
Just a few furnishings and three windows
with wooden shutters outside painted green,
and when the sun hits them and filters through
they give the room an agreeable warmth.
Whenever I go, I find friendly people
conversing discreetly, full of genuine
interest in what they say and hear.
One important detail: they have nothing
to sell, and no product to advertise.

Invitation to Dance

With great difficulty I keep intact
an old outpost that with the passage of time
has been converted into a fortress.
Taking cover behind what I have lost,
with a clear mind I defend the privilege
of being who I am, of writing how I write,
and of living how I live, provided that
my body clings to the bare essentials.
Now that August hammers out its metals
with an impudence that seems excessive,
I seek refuge in the solemnity
that's now a part of me and represents me.
Afterwards, the gods will show me which way
and with whom I will continue on this path;
calm and composed, I will extend my hands
to learn the new rhythm of the rain.

REVIEWS

Scent of the Birthsoil

Chronicles of a Village, by Nguyễn Thanh Hiện,
translated by Quyên Nguyễn-Hoàng, Yale University Press, 2024
Review by Phương Anh Nguyễn

How does one go about recording the scent of a 'birthsoil'? This
question permeates this delicate and poetic novel *Chronicles of a
Village* by Nguyễn Thanh Hiện, translated by Quyên Nguyễn-Hoàng.
In her translator's note, Quyên makes a connection between the idea
of 'scent' and 'birthsoil' through the homonyms of 'hương': one
derives from the character of 香 that could mean 'scent' or 'perfume',
while the other has roots in 鄉, meaning 'village', 'native land' or
'birthsoil'. The idea of the 'scent' is posited as a way to experience
the past; it becomes a force that holds all the seemingly scattered,
unrelated and, at times, contradictory elements of the novel into
something singular. Chimeric and intangible, the scent of the
'birthsoil' assumes the dimensions of a grassroot resistance against
the historical mutilation imposed on the village.

The narrator, a scribe, records the life of his village, the land and
its inhabitants. However, he does not tell a definitive story. As Quyên
notes, these 'moth-eaten memories' are relayed as chronicles to
'eternalise the vanishing beauty'. These memories are told in such a
way that they remain unyielding to a totalising gaze that puts things
into a clear and linear sequence of cause and effect. In the scribe's
history-telling, the past is steadfastly hesitant, shrinking from
revealing too much. Whatever historical truth there may be, it is
interlaced with gossip, legends, edited historical accounts,
conversations, and hearsay. As the narrator's father asserts, 'history
is only a draft copy, son, nothing is certain, nothing is true'.

Rather than attempting to index a conclusive timeline, Nguyễn

Thanh Hiện's story explores a different way to connect all the pieces – past, present, human and non-human – together. Through the practice of oral history, the praxis of genealogy, of simply retracing what has been told through generations without the need to fact-check, the text allows the past to meander. At the same time, the narrator is aware that some kind of other 'history', another timeline is taking place. Under the stewardship of the 'sightless humans', this other history is guided by the chant of 'let's together march forward'.

Amidst this whirlpool of histories, the relation between human and land is maimed. In an unmarked village near the Mun mountains, people have long survived by negotiating and communicating with the soil. Through the character of the father, the person who has taught the scribe much about soil-wisdom, we are told of the bond between 'rice, fabric and poetry', between 'the books and the ploughs'. Some might read this as harking back to an idyllic agrarian culture; however, that is not the case. *Chronicles* want us to simply tune in to our surroundings and notice the connections that are at times invisible.

As I reread the book, I was reminded of Daisy Hilyard's *The Second Body* that proposes the idea of a 'second body' to reconcile with our immediate environment and to make this relationship more tangible, and more embodied. *Chronicles*, too, is proposing a new language: a language in movement, a language that shows us new connections and pushes the reader to widen their empathy. It encourages us to renew our ties to the world through renewing our ties to the past. Justice for this small land means doing justice to its muddied stories, to the animals that live there, to the mountains, and to the ghosts. In a time upended by climate change and environmental rulings, as more and more people are displaced, such language feels urgent.

Chronicles underlines the idea that to refashion history is to refashion our kinship. The scribe may not explicitly state what he feels, nevertheless the language he uses to shape the things he records is indicative of his love, and attachment to the land. He imagines the bygone days as a 'condensation of a thousand-year-long gathering', as a tale akin to 'unconscious poetry', and regards the mountains not just as a slab of earth's flesh, but rather as a 'secret mantra' that holds the bountiful enigmas of existence. The text rejects common punctuation, the capitalised 'I' and the idea of a plot, allowing the pulsing emotions in the sentences' undercurrents, to emerge and to drift. Thus, nestled within *Chronicles of a Village*, between the folds of ecological grief, is a tale of silted-romance, of alluvium-hope for a land maimed by the act of history.

Rhythms of the Soul

Solio, Samira Negrouche
translated by Nancy Naomi Carlson, Seagull Books, 2024
Review by Khadija Aidoo

Solio by Samira Negrouche, translated by Nancy Naomi Carlson from French, takes us on an enlightening journey between the self and the other, redefining notions of time and space. Throughout these lyrical poems, questions of identity, memory, and connection are fluidly evoked and explored.

'All life is movement' is the message that underpins this collection. We are constantly reminded of our duty and destiny to keep moving in order to keep ourselves alive. Reading *Solio* feels like watching a mystifying ballet that pulls you into its whirlwind, moving you from the past to the present, from the Algiers to Gorée, enchanting you all the while. From 'Quay 2|1, A Three-Axis Musical Score', part II':

> I move forward
> in the river moving forward
> I'm rooted in movement
> time passes through me
> beings pass through me
> they are me
> I am them

What is striking about these poetry sequences is their contradictory and disorientating use of language. Negrouche oscillates between the 'I's and 'you's such that the reader is unsure of the key players in the conversation. There is something admirable about this strange diction, in that it works to counter a disengaged, half-alert reading. It keeps us on our toes, preventing us from ever feeling like we completely get the poems. The peculiar tilt of Negrouche's language is recreated in English by Carlson. From 'Quay 2|1, A Three-Axis Musical Score', part II':

> I don't know
> who's speaking
> I can't tell
> who's passing by
> I forget myself
> in the sneezing of daylight

Beyond this unique language, *Solio* stands out for its portrayal of complex interpersonal relationships. Characters often shift between 'guardian' and 'dependent' roles, creating nuanced power dynamics. At some points, the narrator appears vulnerable, particularly when seeking support from the distant 'you' or detailing the attributes of their guardian angel. However, at other times, the narrator takes on a guardian role, looking out for others. Towards the end of the collection, they declare that they 'came from an earlier time | to remind you of the promise of dawn', showing their commitment to safeguarding others. The fluidity of these relationships makes it difficult to categorise them as purely amicable, romantic or parental. Yet, it is also this ambiguity that enhances the universality of *Solio*, allowing us to connect more deeply with the characters and the text. In 'Quay 2|1, A Three-Axis Musical Score', part II', she writes:

> (...) it's so cold
> that I don't hear you anymore
> you said the sea?
> do you want to swim

in the sea?
In a pink and pistachio
Wetsuit?
I'm pretty sure
my guardian angel
is allergic
to pistachios (...)

The vivid nature imagery employed by Negrouche in *Solio*
breathes life into its scenes. The tree's daunting 'verticality'
emphasises its might, while its far-reaching branches symbolise deep
interconnectedness with the environment. Nature is portrayed as
being vital to human survival, with trees acting as record-keepers of
history and preserving the legacies of our predecessors. Sunandini
Banerjee's enchanting illustrations further enhance the effect of the
images. For instance, in 'Traces', she writes: Here there are sacred
souls behind the trunks, the sacred | trunks of the sacred trees, in
the sacred forest you're | passing through.

Another key message within the poetry sequences is that 'all
things pass', good or bad. The sea is often used to represent life's
many fluctuations as in 'Traces', where fierce waves embody
moments of chaos, and the gentle tide embodies the more
tranquil ones:

You let a part of yourself go along with the wave,
you move in the other direction.

The halo of the wave hypnotizes you,
you have no choice but to slow down.

The halo of the wave hypnotizes you,
and this silent cloud seems to carry so many stories, so
    many words, so
many faces, so many landscapes, so many languages, so
very many

There is much emphasis on the fact that these cyclic fluctuations
have persisted for centuries as our ancestors have experienced
them too. We are encouraged to recognise the paths paved by our
predecessors while continuing to carve out our own. Thus, the text
encourages us, once again, to embrace our identity as part of a wider
collective. We are reminded that even the simplest actions, such as
the movement of a finger, become significant when we consider their
universality and their power to connect us with others. From 'Traces':

A finger realigns the threads /// a finger cuts /// a
finger inverts /// a finger presses /// a finger slips ///
a finger goes and comes back /// a finger inverts the
threads /// a finger flits /// a finger gives you a drink
/// a finger pulls fabric over the baby's cheek /// a
finger smiles /// a finger tastes /// a finger measures ///
a finger dips into mercury /// a finger spools threads (...)

Negrouche's writing is dynamic, compelling and deeply engaged,
exploring the raw facets of humanity. *Solio* nourishes the soul, with its
inherent spirituality and musicality, and dances its way gracefully
into the heart.

NOTES ON CONTRIBUTORS

ADAM TAPPER is a student at the University of Chicago Laboratory Schools and co-editor of *Ouroboros Review*, the Schools' translation magazine. He translates German and Yiddish literature and poetry.

ADRIAN NATHAN WEST is an essayist, author of the novel *My Father's Diet*, and a translator from German, Spanish, and Catalan.

AIDAN ROONEY (born in 1965, Ireland) is a teacher, translator and poet. *Go There* (Madhat Press, 2020) is his third collection of poetry. He lives in Hingham, Massachusetts.

AKAISER is the Pushcart Prize-nominated author of <glint> (Milk & Cake Press) and an NEA-awarded translator of Catalan, French & Spanish. *Unnameable*, by Catalan poet Anna Gual, is forthcoming in English (Zephyr Press, 2025). https://akexperiments.org

ÁLVARO FAUSTO TARUMA is a Mozambican poet, born in 1988 in Maputo. His most recent collection of poetry, *Recolher Obrigatório do Coração*, was published in 2022 by Alcance Editores.

ANJA KAMPMANN holds an MFA in poetry and fiction from the German Literature Institute. Kampmann received the Irseer Pegasus Writers Award and has published her writing in numerous magazines and anthologies.

ANNA CROWE is a Scottish poet and translator whose work has received three PBS Choices/Recommendations. She was awarded a Society of Authors Travelling Scholarship in 2005.

ANNA GUAL is one of Catalunya's most vital poetic voices. Her explorations and the singular way she writes them draws in poets, readers, and critics alike. *Innombrable*, translated into English by AKaiser, is forthcoming (Zephyr Press, 2025). https://annagual.cat

ASTRID ALBEN is a poet, translator and commissioning editor for literature in translation at Prototype.

ÀXEL SANJOSÉ was born in Barcelona in 1960 to a Catalan father and a German mother, and has lived in Munich since 1978. He has published five collections of poetry and translated extensively from Catalan and Spanish.

BOHDAN TOKARSKYI is a literary scholar and translator. He is Assistant Professor of Ukrainian Literature and Culture at Harvard University.

CEVAHIR BEDEL has written five books of poetry and other pieces reflecting on the current political situation in her country and community. She has won numerous awards for her work.

CLEMENTINA SUÁREZ (1902–91) has been called 'the legendary matriarch of Honduran letters'. Suárez penned ten poetry collections between 1930 and 1988 and organized creative communities across Central America.

CLYDE MONEYHUN lives in Idaho and Menorca (Spain) and translates contemporary Catalan-language poets including Ponç Pons, Dolors Miquel, Maria-Mercè Marçal, Anna Dodas, and Míriam Cano.

DERK WYNAND is a former editor of *The Malahat Review,* and he taught in the University of Victoria's Department of Writing until 2004. His translations of Dorothea Grünzweig's *Midsummer Cut* (2002) and *Glass Voices lasináänet* (2009) were published by BuschekBooks.

DOROTHEA GRÜNZWEIG, an award-winning German-born poet, translator and essayist, has lived in Finland since 1989. Among her seven collections of poetry, all published by Wallstein Verlag, are *Vom Eisgebreit (Icefielded)* in 2000 and *Plötzlich alles da (All there in a flash)*, 2021.

ERIK SOLVANGER is a doctor and a farmer, and as a poet the author of four poetry collections. His most recent collection is *Why Life Goes Faster in a White Coat.*

FELÍCIA FUSTER (1921, Barcelona-2012, Paris) was a painter, poet, and translator (French, Japanese), who entered the poetry world at sixty-two. Of six published collections, only ten poems existed in English before 2022.

GABRIEL FERRATER (1922–1972) was a poet and translator. Born in Reus, he spent most of his adult life in and around Barcelona, and is a significant influence on modern poetry in Catalan.

GEMMA GORGA has published seven collections of poetry in Catalan, most recently *Mur* (2017) and *Viatge al centre* (2020). She teaches Medieval and Renaissance Spanish Literature at the University of Barcelona.

GRANT AZEVEDO BELEZA-SCHUTZMAN is a poet and translator. His work has appeared in publications including *Rust + Moth*, *The Shore*, *The Inflectionist Review*, *Asymptote*, and *Your Impossible Voice*.

Little is definitively known of the pseudonymous writer **GUNNAR**, other than that beginning in the 1960s they published poetry and prose in *Der Kreis*, a cultural publication for homosexual men.

JEAN D'AMÉRIQUE (born Jean Civilus, 1994, Haïti) is a writer and performer whose work describes the destruction of his native country and its people. He lives in Paris.

Awarded the Nazim Hikmet Poetry Prize, **JEFFREY KAHRS**' poetry, fiction, essays, book reviews and translations have been published in numerous journals.

JOSEP CARNER (1884–1970), the 'Prince of Catalan Poets', was repeatedly nominated for the Nobel Prize. A diplomat loyal to the Spanish Republic, he spent much of his life in exile.

JOSEP CHECA won his first poetry prize in his hometown at the age of fifteen. He has since published more than a dozen poetry collections and won several prestigious awards.

JOSEP LLUÍS AGUILÓ is a Catalan/Mallorcan poet whose work has been published by Arc as *Lunarium*. His extraordinary imagination uses myth and magic to dissect time and human folly.

JP ALLEN's poems and translations have appeared in *Narrative Magazine*, *Hayden's Ferry*, *The Offing*, and elsewhere. He lives in Durham, North Carolina.

Mexican writer and translator **JUDITH SANTOPIETRO** was awarded a residency at the International Writing Program at the University of Iowa in 2022. She was a finalist for the 2020 Sarah Maguire Prize for Poetry in Translation for her book *Tiawanaku*.

KAROLINE BRÆNDJORD is a poet based in Oslo. She attended the Academy of Creative Writing in Hordaland and studied North American Studies and Social Anthropology at the University of Oslo.

KATHLEEN MCNERNEY, a Professor Emerita from West Virginia University, has taught and written about literature, women's studies, and culture and humanities in general. She has translated various genres from Catalan and Castilian into English. She has been awarded several prizes.

KHADIJA AIDOO is a London-born French translator of Ghanaian heritage. She recently completed the National Centre for Writing's Emerging Translator Mentorship with Sarah Ardizzone, which deepened her interest in the interconnection of languages.

Poet, professor, translator **KIM JENSEN**'s books include *The Woman I Left Behind*, *Bread Alone* and *The Only Thing That Matters*. In 2001, she won the Raymond Carver Award for short fiction.

KLEIN VOORHEES is a writer, artist, and translator. Their work is featured or forthcoming in *Southeast Review*, *North American Review*, and *The Arkansas International*. Find more at www.kleinvoorhees.com

LOURDES MANYÉ is a researcher, and translator from Barcelona, and Professor at Furman University. She has translated the Catalan poet Miquel Martí i Pol and published *Vacation Notebook* and around thirty other translations of his poems in literary journals.

MARIA ANTÒNIA SALVÀ (1869–1958) is generally credited with helping to bring literary Catalan into the modern era, renewing and refreshing the language with poems written in colloquial language about everyday subjects.

MARIA-MERCÈ MARÇAL (1952–1998) was a monumental figure in modern Catalan literature, publishing prolifically across her tragically short life; editing and printing the work of other writers; and delivering countless addresses at gatherings of writers, cultural critics, and feminist activists.

METE ÖZEL is a Turkish writer and translator whose poems, essays and translations have appeared in many Turkish journals. He is a founding partner of an international translation company.

MARIALENA CARR, a former research oceanographer, has translations in *Hyperion*, *Metamorphoses*, *The Common* (forthcoming), and *EL JO-ULL/ THE I-EYE* (2022).

MATTHEW GEDEN is a poet and translator living in Ireland. His collections include *The Cloud Architect* (Doire Press, 2022) and *Ocean of Earth* (SurVision Books, 2024) selected translations of Apollinaire.

MERCÈ RODOREDA (1908–1983), the great Catalan novelist, spent a brief, intense period writing poetry. Following years of exile in France and Switzerland she returned, recognised and esteemed, to Catalonia.

MIQUEL MARTI i POL (1929–2003) lived in Roda de Ter (Catalonia, Spain) and is the most widely read poet in contemporary Catalan literature. He won the Premi d'Honor de les Lletres Catalanes in 1991, the most important literary award in Catalan literature.

NIALL O'GALLAGHER (1981–) is the author of three books of poetry in Gaelic published by CLÀR and of *Fuaimean Gràidh/The Sounds of Love: Selected Poems* (Francis Boutle, 2023).

NINA MURRAY is a Ukrainian-American poet and translator. Her most recent poetry collection is *«Gannota»* (The Braag, 2024).

OSIP MANDELSTAM (1891–1938) wrote these poems in 1937 while in internal exile in Voronezh. The Voronezh poetry has what Joseph Brodsky calls 'incredible psychic acceleration' in the face of impending death.

PAU GASOL VALLS (1978, Barcelona) has been working professionally as an illustrator for a few years. He has experience in various fields (poster design, advertising, web, books), but the precarious nature of illustrators in Spain forces him to combine his craft with other jobs. He is currently working as a bookseller.

PHƯƠNG ANH NGUYỄN is a translator and writer from Việt Nam, with works featured on *Asymptote*, *PR&TA*, *SAND* and in *Here Was Once The Sea: An Anthology of Southeast Asian Ecowriting*.

RACHEL RANKIN is a poet, translator, researcher and Norwegian-language tutor based in Edinburgh. She holds a PhD in Scandinavian Studies from the University of Edinburgh.

REBECCA SIMPSON is based in Barcelona. Her work on Mercè Rodoreda's poetry is an ongoing project. These translations received support from the Translators Programme of the Institut Ramon Llull, Catalonia.

RICHARD DOVE was born in Bath in 1954, and has lived in Munich since 1987. He has published poetry in German and English, while translating, mostly from German (interalia Friederike Mayröcker and Reiner Kunze).

RONALD PUPPO (San Francisco, 1954), award-winning Catalan–English translator and ALTA mentor, has published widely. His full-length version of the Catalan classic Atlantis came out recently at Fum d'Estampa.

ROXANA CRISÓLOGO is a prolific Peruvian-Finnish poet and the founder of Sivuvalo Platform, a multilingual literature association in Helsinki. Her most recent books are *Kauneus: la belleza* and *Dónde Dejar Tanto Ruido*.

SAKTHI JOTHI, a social worker by occupation, is the author of thirteen books of poetry and two essay collections. She is the founder of Sri Sakthi Social, Economic and Educational Welfare Trust.

SHARON DOLIN has translated two books from Catalan: *Book of Minutes* (2019) and *Late to the House of Words: Selected Poems by Gemma Gorga* (2021), winner of Saturnalia's Malinda A. Markham Translation Prize.

SÍLVIA AYMERICH-LEMOS is a poet, novelist, translator and cross-cultural literary activist. Trained in several languages, with a degree in biology, she brings a diversified background to her writing. Her poetry has appeared in international anthologies and reviews.

THILA VARGHESE is a writer and translator based in London, Canada, where she works part-time as a Senior Writing Advisor at Western University. Her translations of Tamil literary works have been published in international magazines and journals.

TÒNIA PASSOLA, a native of Barcelona, is an internationally acclaimed poet. Translated into a dozen languages, her works have garnered prestigious awards at home and abroad.

Before retirement, **TONY BRINKLEY** taught in the English Department at the University of Maine. He is co-editor (with Keith Hanley) of *Romantic Revisions* (Cambridge University Press).

VASYL STUS (1938–1985) was one of Ukraine's most significant twentieth-century poets, and a prolific translator from several languages. As a Ukrainian dissident in the Soviet Union, he spent the last thirteen years of his life in the gulag, where he wrote his magnum opus *Palimpsests* (1980).

WAYNE COX, professor at Anderson University (SC), is a Fulbright and NEA fellow, has appeared in *Poetry* and *Shenandoah,* and published *Things We Leave Behind* (96 Press). His most recent translations appeared in *Metamorphoses* in 2023.